Legends of the Game

LEVEL 7
/g/

Teaching Tips

Turquoise Level 7

This book focuses on the grapheme **/g/**.

Before Reading

- Discuss the title. Ask readers what they think the book will be about. Have them support their answer.
- Ask readers to sort the words on page 3. Read the words together. Reinforce that /g/ can have a hard /g/ sound or a soft /j/ sound.

Read the Book

- Encourage readers to read independently, either aloud or silently to themselves.
- Prompt readers to break down unfamiliar words into units of sound and string the sounds together to form the words. Then, ask them to look for context clues to see if they can figure out what these words mean. Discuss new vocabulary to confirm meaning.
- Urge readers to point out when the focused phonics grapheme appears in the text. Does it have a hard /g/ sound or a soft /j/ sound?

After Reading

- Ask readers comprehension questions about the book. In what ways were people in the book participating in sports?
- Encourage readers to think of other words with the /g/ grapheme. On a separate sheet of paper, have them write the words into two columns: one under the hard /g/ sound and the other under the soft /j/ sound.

© 2024 Booklife Publishing
This edition is published by arrangement with Booklife Publishing.

North American adaptations © 2024 Jump!
5357 Penn Avenue South
Minneapolis, MN 55419
www.jumplibrary.com

Decodables by Jump! are published by Jump! Library.
All rights reserved. No part of this book may be reproduced in any form without written permission from the publisher.

Library of Congress Cataloging-in-Publication Data is available at www.loc.gov or upon request from the publisher.

ISBN: 979-8-88996-876-4 (hardcover)
ISBN: 979-8-88996-877-1 (paperback)
ISBN: 979-8-88996-878-8 (ebook)

Photo Credits
Images are courtesy of Shutterstock.com. With thanks to Getty Images, Thinkstock Photo and iStockphoto. Cover – Leonard Zhukovsky. 4–5 – Jacob Lund, wavebreakmedia. 6–7 – Tom Pennington, Dokshin Vlad. 8–9 – A.PAES, papai. 10–11 – Leonard Zhukovsky. 12–13 – Scott Meivogel, Tinseltown. 14–15 – Andrew Makedonsk, Master1305. 16 – Shutterstock.

Can you sort these words into two groups?
One group has **g** as in **dog**. One group has
g as in **gem**.

ginger

goal

Egypt

energy

grain

regret

page

anger

If you are considered a legend in a sport, you will have tried things that no one could have imagined. You will never be in danger of being forgotten.

Whether it is basketball, hockey, soccer, or swimming, each sport has legends spoken about far and wide.

Being a good sports player is all about fine margins. This means making sure you are at least one percent better each time you play.

Lionel Messi is one of the best soccer players of all time. He was born in Argentina, which is in South America. As a teenager, he went to Spain.

Lots of soccer fans like to say that Messi has magic in his shoes. He is quick and agile. Some say that he makes other players look rigid in comparison.

Messi is treated like a god in Argentina. Whether it is on a digital screen or on a generic wall in a town, you can see things dedicated to Messi.

Serena and Venus Williams are legends of tennis. They have won a huge number of matches and awards. Not just that, they are sisters too!

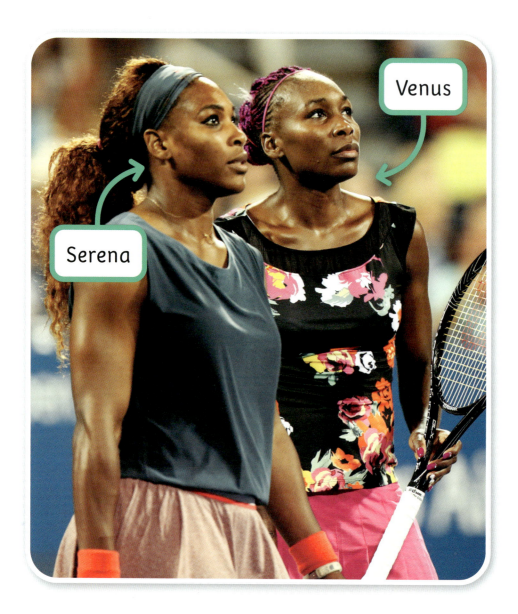

They have often played together as partners. As sisters, they get along well together when they play. Serena has won a huge number of Grand Slams.

LeBron James is not just a gigantic name in basketball. He is a real giant! Like most basketball players, LeBron is tall. He has the skill to match.

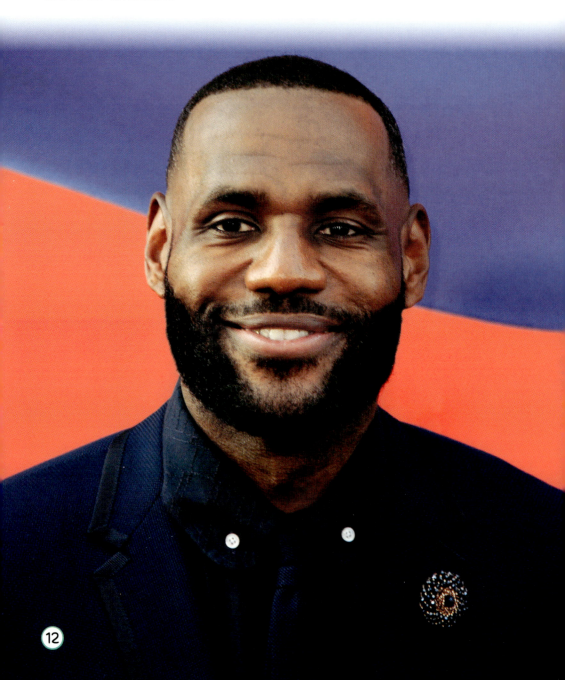

LeBron is one of the most versatile players in basketball. He even has a cool nickname. He is called King James!

Lots of people think that you need to be a genius to win on the biggest stages in sports. That is not correct.

To be a legend of the game, you need to do just one thing: try hard. Never stop practicing, and always push to be the best you can be.

Say the name of each object below. Is the "g" in each a /g/ sound or a /j/ sound?